DODD, MEAD WONDER BOOKS

Wonders of the Weather by Tex Antoine
Wonders of Animal Migration by Jacquelyn Berrill
Wonders of the Fields and Ponds at Night by Jacquelyn Berrill
Wonders of the Woods and Desert at Night by Jacquelyn Berrill
Wonders of the Seashore by Jacquelyn Berrill
Wonders of the Woodland Animals by Jacquelyn Berrill
Wonders of the Wild by Jacquelyn Berrill
Wonders of the Antarctic by Jacquelyn Berrill
Wonders of the Arctic by Jacquelyn Berrill
Wonders of the Tree World by Margaret Cosgrove
Wonders of Your Senses by Margaret Cosgrove
The Wonders Inside You by Margaret Cosgrove
Wonders Under a Microscope by Margaret Cosgrove
Wonders at Your Feet by Margaret Cosgrove
Wonders of the Bird World by Helen Gere Cruickshank
Wonders of the Reptile World by Helen Gere Cruickshank
Wonders of the Rivers by Virginia S. Eifert
Wonders of Mathematics by Rocco Feravolo
Wonders of Sound by Rocco Feravolo
Wonders of the Heavens by Kenneth Heuer
Wonders of Animal Architecture by Sigmund A. Lavine
Wonders of Animal Disguises by Sigmund A. Lavine
Wonders of the Anthill by Sigmund A. Lavine
Wonders of the Aquarium by Sigmund A. Lavine
Wonders of the Beetle World by Sigmund A. Lavine
Wonders of the Hive by Sigmund A. Lavine
Wonders of the Wasp's Nest by Sigmund A. Lavine
Wonders of the Dinosaur World by William H. Matthews III
Wonders of Snow and Ice by Christie McFall
Wonders of Gems by Richard M. Pearl
Wonders of Rocks and Minerals by Richard M. Pearl
Wonders of Hummingbirds by Hilda Simon
Wonders of the Butterfly World by Hilda Simon
Wonders of Our National Parks by Peter Thomson
Wonders of the World Between the Tides by Norman Hammond Wakeman
Wonders of Flight by Robert Wells
Wonders of the Dog World by Leon F. Whitney, D.V.M.
Wonders of the Deep Sea by Boris Arnov, Jr.,
    and Helen Mather-Smith Mindlin
Wonders of the Ocean Zoo by Boris Arnov, Jr.,
    and Helen Mather-Smith Mindlin

Other books written and illustrated by Hilda Simon

WONDERS OF THE BUTTERFLY WORLD

THE YOUNG PATHFINDER'S BOOK OF BIRDS

THE STUDY OF BIRDS MADE SIMPLE

THE YOUNG PATHFINDER'S BOOK OF SNAKES

EXPLORING THE WORLD OF SOCIAL INSECTS

Wonders of
Hummingbirds

BY HILDA SIMON

Illustrated by the author

DODD, MEAD & COMPANY, NEW YORK

To my mother, in whose California rose garden
I watched my first hummingbirds

Contents

Fragments of the Rainbow

"Of all animated beings, the hummingbird is the most elegant in form, the most brilliant in color. The precious stones and metals to which our art only lends polish are not to be compared to this gem of Nature, whose masterpiece the little bird represents. She has loaded it with all the gifts of which she has given other birds only a share . . . The emerald, the ruby, the topaz glitter in its plumage, which is never sullied by the dust of ground."

In this poetic fashion did the Comte de Buffon, a French naturalist of the eighteenth century, give expression to his delight after observing hummingbirds in South America. His colleagues from other countries joined him in praising the beauty and daintiness of these little birds. John James Audubon, the famous American naturalist and artist, thought that there could not be a person who would not pause and wonder on seeing "this lovely little fragment of the rainbow moving on humming winglets through the air, suspended as if by magic in it, flitting from one flower to another, with motions that are as light as they are airy . . ."

And Charles Waterton, the English naturalist, found the hummingbird family to be "adorned with plumage of such amazing brilliancy as to compete with, if not surpass, the united splendor of our most precious stones themselves . . . Though least in size, the glittering mantle of the hummingbird entitles it to the first place in the list of birds in the New World. It may truly be called the bird of Paradise . . . It is now a ruby—now a topaz—now an emerald —now all burnished gold!"

From these descriptions, it becomes clear how easily the observer gets carried away by the unusual beauty of these tiny birds. All the more surprising is the fact that no common name has been found for them which gives some indication of the glittering colors with which they are adorned, and which call forth extravagant praise from all observers, expert and layman alike. One would think that someone would have come up with a name such as "jewel birds" or "rainbow birds," instead of the rather uninspired "hummingbirds."

The scientific names of the individual kinds, or species, do a better job of describing them. Zoologists have used up practically every gem and precious stone, plus the sun and the stars, in the Latin names used to designate hummingbirds. We find combinations meaning "fiery topaz," "golden torch," "sapphire," "crimson topaz," and many others.

The Indians in the regions where hummingbirds are most abundant—Central and South America—have shown an often remarkable talent for poetic word pictures in selecting names for the beautiful little creatures. Indian names such as "rays of the sun," "tresses of the day-star," and many others all prove to what an extent hummingbirds have managed to arouse admiration in the legends the Indians tell about the little birds, legends in which frequently astonishing and unique feats are attributed to the tiny

Bright emerald green of this hummingbird's plumage—a structural color—may appear quite black when seen from a different angle.

glittering creatures.

The beauty of the gleaming, metallic, and iridescent or rainbowlike feathers found in many—but not all—hummingbirds results from the fact that these colors seem to glow with a life of their own, and to change their hue with every shift of position or angle of light. You may be looking at a perching hummingbird, for instance, and admiring its golden-greenish "bib." But let the bird suddenly turn its head, and the green changes into pure burnished gold, and then into glowing copper. Another turn, and, as if by magic, the color has disappeared altogether, only to reappear in all its brightness with the bird's next movement. No other small bird can boast of such brilliance in coloring, although many other birds have iridescent colors that give off a rainbowlike change of hues.

What makes these metallic colors not only beautiful, but also most interesting, is the fact that they are not caused by any chem-

9

The glittering red throat of the ruby-throat is a physical, or structural, color.

The bright "flat" red of the cardinal is a chemical, or pigmented, color.

ical substance as are, for instance, the bright red of the cardinal, the orange of the oriole, and the yellow of the canary. All these colors are due to *pigments*, coloring substances, that are found in the feathers. You are all familiar with such coloring matter, for it is much the same kind as found in the paints and the dyes we use in our everyday life.

Pigments can be extracted from the feathers that contain them by treating the latter with certain chemicals. If the feather of a cardinal is so treated, the results will be a reddish solution—and a colorless feather.

Nothing like that, however, would happen if you treated an iridescent hummingbird feather in this way. The color may disappear as long as the feather is wet, but as soon as it dries, the colors will reappear in their original strength and brilliance. The reason for the different reaction of the hummingbird feather to the chemical is found in the fact that its colors are created, not by any chemical coloring matter, but solely by the play of light on the peculiar construction of the feather.

To understand this, we have to keep in mind that white light is made up of many different brilliant colors, the entire range of which is called the *spectrum.* You probably have seen what happens when a beam of white light is sent through a glass prism. The light is bent and broken up into the various colors of which it is composed, with red at one end of the scale, and violet at the opposite end. The other colors—orange, yellow, green, and blue—are graded in between in that order.

Metallic hummingbird feathers have a special construction, the surface being covered with a mosaic of thin transparent films, which bend and reflect certain colors of the spectrum. Whether blue, green, red, or yellow is reflected is determined largely by the thickness of the films, and also by the angle at which the light strikes them. In addition, all the hollow parts of the fine feather branches are filled with a black substance called *melanin.* This black backing enhances the strength of the reflected color, and absorbs the other colors. The result is the pure spectral hues of the hummingbird's iridescence.

Keeping in mind the origin of these colors, it is now easy to see

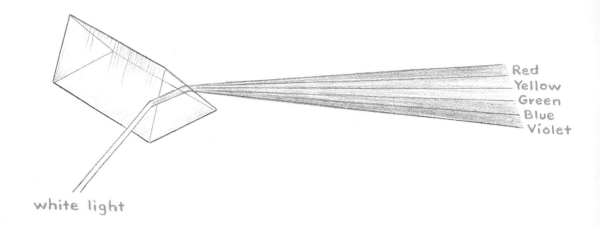

Red
Yellow
Green
Blue
Violet

white light

The spectrum, a continuous band of colors, results from the bending of white light.

why they disappear when the light is not right, for they *are* light, not substance. When the light *is* right, though, the colors glow and glitter with a purity and brilliance that is unique, and cannot be matched by any other member of the bird world, for no other bird has feathers that are constructed in quite the same way as are those of hummingbirds.

The fact that the hummingbird feather does not depend upon a chemical substance for its color also explains why these feathers are "colorfast"—that is, why they do not tend to fade the way pigment colors do. We all know from experience that the colors and dyes we are familiar with in our daily life often fade rather quickly, especially if they are exposed to bright light. Drapes, for instance, and textiles in general, lose much of their color over a period of time. This happens because the chemical substance responsible for the color changes through exposure to light. The same thing, incidentally, happens to many mounted birds whose feathers contain pigment colors, as one can frequently observe in

12

mounted specimens in museums. Some of these colors fade so quickly that zoologists sometimes are forced to restore the natural color pattern artificially by painting the faded feathers.

No such trouble develops with mounted hummingbirds. Their colors stay as bright and glittering years after their death as they ever were in life. This, of course, is due to the fact that these colors are based, not upon chemical coloring matter, but on the reflection of spectral colors by the structural peculiarities of the feathers. It follows that only if and when the structure that creates these colors is damaged or destroyed do the colors disappear. If, for instance, you crush a hummingbird feather so completely that the thin transparent films are ruined, you will find that in the same moment the brilliant metallic colors are gone forever, and what remains of the feather appears blackish. On the other hand, crushing a feather containing pigment will not affect the color in any way. No matter how mangled, it still will retain its original hue.

The best way to see and admire hummingbirds is, of course, to see them alive. Many zoos now have a collection of these attractive little creatures, and the visitor can observe them as they flit around in their glass cages, flashing the brilliant colors for which they have become famous. But even the mounted specimens in the museums will give you an idea of the beauty and daintiness of these birds, and it will take not too great an effort to see why they have been compared to the sun, the stars, the rainbow, and all the precious stones most coveted by man.

Hummingbird Country

When we look at the huge class of birds, with its twenty-odd orders and hundreds of families—a family in this case being a subdivision of an order—we find that the majority is represented in various parts of the world. Members of the duck and goose family, for instance, are found in Europe, Asia, the Americas, and Africa. The same applies to pigeons and doves, many songbirds, and scores of other bird families. It does not, however, apply to hummingbirds. This family is found exclusively in the Western Hemisphere, in North America, but especially in South and Central America as well as the adjacent islands, such as Cuba and Jamaica. Not a single species of hummingbird is found anywhere else in the world.

The real heartland of "hummingbird country" is the region close to the equator in South America. Ecuador, which was named after this imaginary dividing line, is the home of more than 150 species —or roughly half the known number—of hummingbirds. Colombia also can claim a great number of different kinds. Moving away from this center—regardless of whether one goes north or south —they become less abundant, even though more than 100 species are still found in central South America, especially Brazil, and almost 60 in Central America.

As we get farther and farther away from the equator, the number of species decreases rapidly. In northern Mexico, for instance, close to the border to the United States, only about 20 kinds of hummingbirds have been observed. The corresponding latitudes in South America can claim about twice the number, but when we

NORTH AMERICA

West Indies

Equator

SOUTH AMERICA

Map of the Americas showing distribution and range of hummingbirds. Greatest number are found in solid-color areas. Only a single species frequents those areas dotted in black.

come to Patagonia, at the southern tip of the continent, we find only a single species. Even this is astonishing, though, for as hummingbirds are primarily creatures of the tropics and subtropics, one would not expect to find one of their kind in a climate as cold and inhospitable as that of Patagonia—nor, of course, at the other end of the hemisphere, in Alaska, where another enterprising species is found. The fact is that wherever flowers still bloom in the Americas, at least one kind of hummingbird is apt to turn up.

Additional proof that these little birds are extremely adaptable can be found in the great variety of habitats which the individual members of the family have chosen for themselves. Some live in regions of steaming jungles, rain forests, and tropical heat. Others like clear, cool mountain air; still others prefer the dry heat of deserts and plains.

One of the most brilliantly colorful and glittering of all hummingbirds, the crimson topaz, makes its home in the jungles of

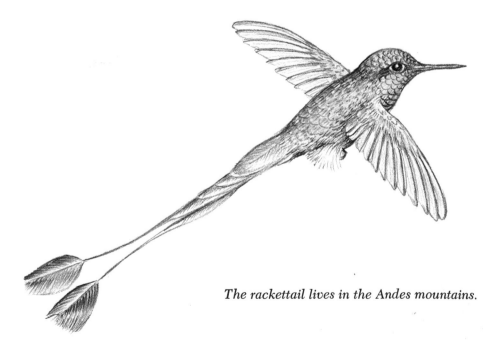

The rackettail lives in the Andes mountains.

The Chimborazan Hill Star is found only on Mount Chimborazo.

Venezuela and British Guiana, spending most of its time high up in the treetops, where it finds an abundant supply of nectar-rich blossoms. Getting a close-up look at this bird is a rewarding experience, for its body gleams in various shades of iridescent gold, copper, and red.

Many hummingbirds like to live in mountainous regions. The largest member of the family, appropriately named *Patagona gigas*, or Patagonian giant, ranges the Andes mountains of South America. Another hummingbird of the Andes is the tiny rackettail, which has two elongated tail feathers with flaglike tips.

The champion of all mountain-dwelling species, however, is a handsome purple-collared bird that makes its home at altitudes of up to 15,000 feet—just below the snow line—on Mount Chimborazo

17

Giant hummingbird, shown in life size,
measures eight inches from bill to tail.

Tiny "bee" hummingbird (life size) measures only two inches from bill to tail.

in Ecuador. It it appropriately called the "Chimborazo bird," for it is found nowhere else except on that one mountain peak.

As a rule, hummingbirds do not migrate far, and many stay in the same location all year round. However, there are some notable exceptions to this rule, and at least two of them compensate for the non-migratory habits of their relatives by being real long-distance travelers. One of these migratory hummingbirds is the ruby-throat, a species that breeds in the eastern half of the North American continent. The other is the rufous hummingbird, a western species that goes as far north as Alaska. Twice a year these hummingbirds make a 2,000-mile journey in which they exchange the sub-tropical climate of their Central American winter home for the cooler temperatures of North America.

It is interesting to note the tremendous variations in the range of the individual species. Many non-migratory hummingbirds have an extended range, meaning that they are found over a large geographical area. The aforementioned rackettail, for instance, is found all the way from Bolivia to Venezuela. In sharp contrast, other hummingbirds are limited to a tiny area—a mountain peak, as in the case of the Chimborazo bird, or a small island. Examples of the latter are the pennant-tailed *Trochylus polytmus*, which lives only in Jamaica, or the tiny "bee" hummingbird, *Calypte helenae*, whose home is Cuba and the Isle of Pines.

Luckily, hummingbirds—even though it may be only one species —can be found in practically every part of the South as well as the North American continent. The beautiful little birds, with their glittering colors and interesting ways, are an attraction for any place where they make their home, and we therefore should be grateful for the fact that, to varying degrees, the entire Western world is "hummingbird country."

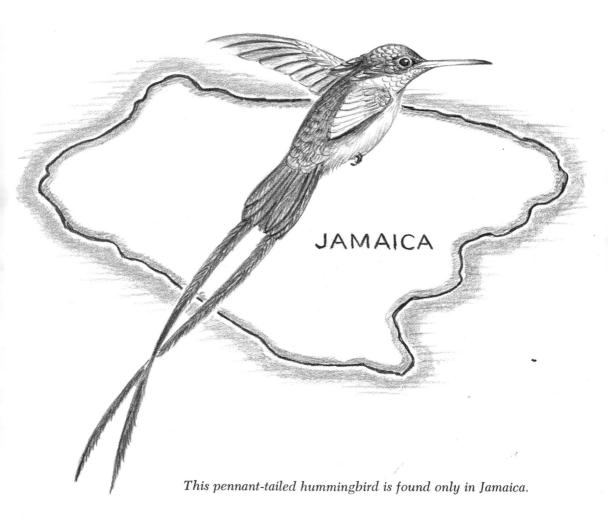

JAMAICA

This pennant-tailed hummingbird is found only in Jamaica.

Life and Habits

Among the many tales told by Indians about hummingbirds is one that describes how the tobacco monopoly, held and jealously guarded many years back by the people of Trinidad, was finally broken by the Indians of Venezuela. After long deliberation on how to get hold of the priceless seed, they decided to send a hummingbird, riding on the back of a stork, in the hope that the tiny fellow would manage to grab a seed and bring it safely back. The strategy was successful—the hummingbird returned to Venezuela in triumph with the seed!

Even though this is just a fable, it illustrates the fact that the Indians correctly judged fearlessness to be one of the hummingbird's outstanding characteristics. As a rule, these tiny birds are neither shy nor easily frightened. On the contrary, they will not hesitate to take on an adversary many times their own size. In this, as in many other ways, they differ markedly from most other birds.

Hummingbirds belong to an order—in zoological classification, a group below the class, but above the family—of birds with the scientific name *Apodiformes*, the literal translation of which is "without feet." Only two families, hummingbirds and swifts, make up this order. While these birds do have feet, of course, they are so small and weak that they can be used only for perching, or for clinging to rough surfaces, but not for walking around on the ground. To the layman, the feet are about the only point of resemblance between a swift and a hummingbird, for otherwise they look anything but related to each other. Swifts, of which there are roughly 400 species, are found in many parts of the world. The

Long, slender bills enable hummingbirds to reach deep into flowers for their liquid food.

United States has only four kinds. Brownish or soot-colored birds that superficially resemble swallows with their long, sickle-shaped wings and tiny, widely-slit beaks, swifts look as different as possible from the usually bright-colored, needle-billed hummingbirds. Zoologists, however, determine relationship on the basis, not of appearance, but of certain body structures, and have concluded that swifts are indeed the hummingbirds' nearest relatives.

Somewhere along the line, a long time back, hummingbirds evolved their own special ways of life, habits, and modes of flight. The latter especially are unique. Athough many birds are strong and wonderful fliers, no other bird in the world can match the aerial acrobatics that a hummingbird can—and does—perform as part of its daily routine.

Swifts also are excellent, graceful fliers. They have to be, for they catch their food, which consists of insects, on the wing. However, they lack the peculiar wing structure which makes humming-birds such superior aerialists.

It is believed that evolution of hummingbirds as a special group started when, sometime in the gray past, these birds began to pursue their insect prey right into the blossoms in which the latter often sought refuge. In this way, the theory goes, did the ancestors of today's hummingbirds find that the sweet flower nectar was quite a delectable food.

Whatever it was that started the ancestral hummingbirds on the road toward specialization as nectar feeders, the fact remains that the modern birds are uniquely equipped for this way of life. The modification of their wing structure—about which we shall hear more in another chapter—gives them a maneuverability no other bird possesses, so that, among other things, hummingbirds can hover like a miniature helicopter while feeding from a flower.

Tubular tongue of hummingbird, forked at the tip, allows it to suck nectar from blossoms.

The adaptations of the hummingbird's bill and tongue are other examples of their specialized evolution. To reach and draw out the nectar which is found at the base of very long-necked blossoms, hummingbirds developed a long, thin, needlelike bill, and a tubular tongue which can be extended far beyond the tip of the bill.

With the help of these instruments, the birds can reach and pump out the nectar even from the most long-necked flowers.

It is interesting to find that further specialization of the bill occurs in individual species. It may be sickle-shaped, awl-shaped, up- or down-curved, depending upon the kinds of flowers the birds primarily feed on.

Nectar, of course, is not the hummingbirds' sole diet. They could not exist on sugar alone. By eating small insects and spiders, they add the necessary protein to their diet. The insects are picked up from the flowers, or from leaves and bark. Hummingbirds also often snap up insects in mid-air, and one species punctures the base of flowers to catch the insects hidden inside.

By penetrating deep inside the flower with its tongue, the hummingbird often inadvertently dispenses pollen, thus fertilizing the plant and enabling it to reproduce. This service is usually performed by insects, the most famous pollinator being the honeybee,

Specialized bill of sword-bearer is longer than bird's body.

and the hummingbird is the only New World bird that takes over this insect role.

It seems that red is the favorite color of most hummingbirds. Not only do they seem to prefer visiting red flowers, but it has been ob-

Specialization of bill is also shown by the sickle-bill.

served that they are interested in all red objects, investigating them to see whether they will yield any food.

The tremendous energy output demanded by the hummingbird's way of life calls for large amounts of food—fuel to keep the engine running, so to speak. To understand this, we must keep in mind that the hummingbird spends most of its waking hours on the wing, zooming and darting around with rapidly beating wings, and pausing to rest only for short intervals. Such activity burns up energy at a tremendous rate, and accordingly constant "refueling" is necessary. It has been calculated that if a man were to use up as much energy as does a hummingbird, he would have to consume about 300 pounds of food per day! A hummingbird's food, which consists mainly of nectar with a sugar content of 20 per cent, can supply much more energy than can the average human diet. Still, the bird has to consume something like half its weight in sugar every day to get the energy it needs for its active life. For this reason, hummingbirds eat every fifteen minutes or so, which adds up to a total of approximately 50 meals a day. This explains why they have to spend a great part of the day searching for flowers that can supply nectar, the mainstay of their diet.

If food should be scarce, hummingbirds have to conserve energy. They seem to do this during their sleep, sinking into a state of torpor, or suspended animation, during which their body temperature drops from about 100 to 64 degrees. In this state they are sluggish and numb, and can be picked up and handled without difficulty. When food is plentiful, though, they sleep in a normal fashion.

Their superb flying powers are directly connected with the hummingbirds' characteristic fearlessness, curiosity, and fighting spirit. A hummingbird will investigate anything that arouses its curiosity, including humans. They often fly within a few feet of a man, and have been observed to feed from the hand, or even perch on a finger. This does not mean, however, that hummingbirds have any special affection for humans; what it does mean is that they feel confident of their ability to get out of any tight situation that may develop.

For the same reason, hummingbirds will unhesitatingly engage in battles with much larger animals—and usually drive them away.

Two male hummingbirds engage in a spirited fight.

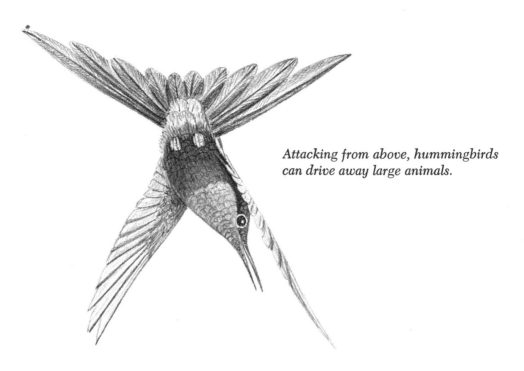

Attacking from above, hummingbirds can drive away large animals.

They seem to be aware that any chances of their being caught by their adversary are extremely slim, and this appears to be true. In these battles, the hummingbird dives down from above at its foe, aiming for the head. Although actual physical contact is not often made during these encounters, having this little streak of feathered fury with a needle-sharp bill coming down in a power dive is usually not the other animal's idea of fun, regardless of whether it happens to be another bird, a reptile, or a mammal. In most cases, therefore, the larger animal retreats ignominiously, and the hummingbird remains victorious on the field of battle.

It is common practice for male birds to defend the territory they have staked out for themselves against intruders, especially other male birds. Here, again, however, hummingbirds are more pugnacious than other members of their class. It seems almost as though they enjoy fighting for the sake of the sport, and they will do battle

Beauty of form and color make up for hummingbirds' lack of vocal talents.

with another member of their own kind on the slightest provocation.

While hummingbirds are beautiful to look at, their voices in no way match their appearance. A hummingbird cannot sing in the sense that a songbird sings. Its voice is usually heard only when the bird is angry, and consists of a chatter which can hardly be called melodious. Vocal performance, then, is the one gift hummingbirds did not receive from Nature, but their beautiful appearance and interesting characteristics fully make up for this deficiency.

When mating time arrives, the male hummingbird puts on a spectacular show for the benefit of the female of his choice. For this performance, the female perches on a branch or twig not far from the ground. The male then rises high into the air, and dives right in front of the female, executing a number of precise arcs and loops around her. Although there are variations in the courtship practices of individual species, most male hummingbirds perform similar aerial acrobatics in an effort to impress the female. In addition, her perch has been chosen in a way that lets the light strike the male's iridescent feathers at just the right angle, with the result that the metallic colors of these feathers glitter with full brilliance during the bird's performance, which is repeated until the female, dazzled by the combination of acrobatics plus gleaming colors, is ready to succumb to the male's charms.

With the help of high-speed cameras, much has been learned, especially in the last few decades, about the ways and habits of hummingbirds. Much, however, still is unknown and remains to be learned. Nobody, for instance, knows the exact lifespan of a hummingbird, although individual birds are reported to have lived twelve years. Future observation and study is certain to add many more interesting details to our present knowledge of the life and habits of these charming little creatures.

Nests, Eggs, and Young

As soon as one female has been wooed and won, the male goes on to dazzle others with his display of glittering colors and aerial gymnastics. The female he has left behind in the meantime goes about building a nest. Sad to say, there is no question of the male sharing this task with her, nor does he later on, except in rare instances, take any part in incubating the eggs, and feeding and protecting the young, as do so many other male birds. The female, however, seems fully capable of coping with the job of raising a family.

Hummingbird nests come in a variety of shapes and forms, and may be found in almost any location except on the ground. In many cases, the nests are masterpieces of craftsmanship, fashioned with much care and patience. Take for instance the nest of the ruby-throated hummingbird, a species that breeds in the eastern part of North America. The cup-shaped structure, which is not much larger than a big walnut, often is found straddling a branch.

31

It is made of grasses, moss, plant fibers and plant down, lined with spiderwebs, and decorated on the outside with lichens, the dry, flowerless plants that grow on tree bark and rocks. The nest is thus well camouflaged and may look like a big bump in the branch.

Some hummingbirds use their saliva to glue the nesting materials together, a habit they have in common with their relatives, the swifts. The nest of one kind of swift, in fact, is made entirely of hardened saliva! Hummingbirds do not do anything like that, but some that live high up in the mountains glue their nests to the side of a rock, using saliva to fasten it securely to the vertical surface.

Many hummingbird nests are cup-shaped, and either saddle a branch, or are tucked away in the crotch of a bush or tree. Others are bag-shaped, and may be suspended from a hanging vine, or atttached to pendant leaves. In such cases, all evidence points to the fact that the hummingbird builds the entire nest on the wing, weaving the materials together while hovering before the nesting site. At least one female who was observed displayed considerable ingenuity in balancing the nest which she had built and which was hanging, fastened by only one spot on its rim, from a long thin line. Curious about why the nest was hanging horizontally, instead of being tipped over to one side, the naturalist who had been watching the female investigated, and found that she had built little clay "bricks" into the bottom of the nest, thus neatly balancing the structure!

When the nest is finished, the female lays two white eggs. The number hardly ever seems to vary, no matter what the species. Neither does the color—hummingbird eggs are always white and unmarked. Although they are small, of course, generally about the size of peas, they are relatively large compared to the size of the bird. The "bee" hummingbird of Cuba, for instance, lays eggs that are only a quarter of an inch long, but then the entire length of the bird is only two inches, of which one-third is taken up by the bill.

Incubation time, the period during which the mother has to warm the eggs, seems to be about two weeks for most species. When the baby hummingbirds hatch, they are blackish in color, naked, blind—and constantly hungry, like all baby birds. Feeding two ever-demanding mouths as well as herself means that the mother hummingbird has to be on the wing searching for food from dawn to dusk.

Female ruby-throat with her nest and eggs

During the first few days, the young are fed a diet of high protein content, consisting of small insects and spiders. Later, the mother starts to feed them the nectar which from then on will remain their chief food throughout life. Transporting the sweet

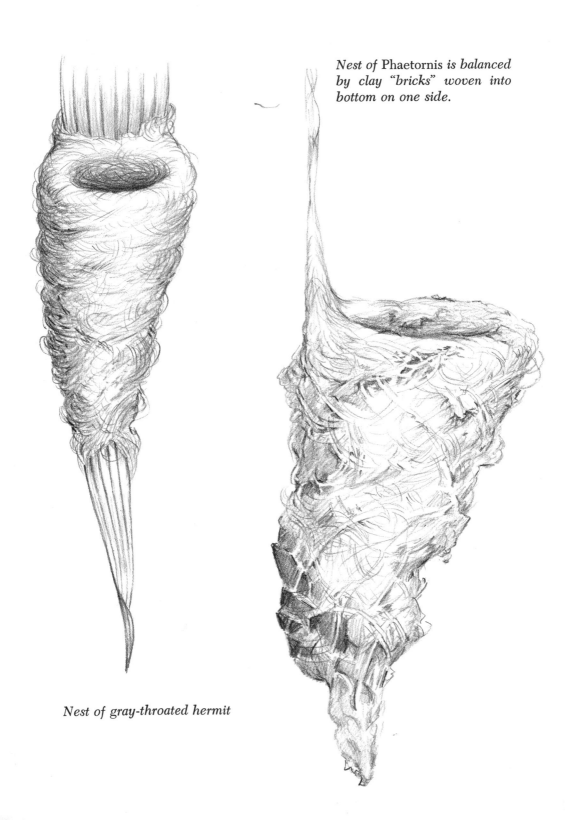

Nest of Phaetornis is balanced by clay "bricks" woven into bottom on one side.

Nest of gray-throated hermit

liquid to the nest would seem to present something of a problem, but the mother hummer overcomes this by simply swallowing the nectar and storing it in her crop—a baglike enlargement of the gullet found in many birds.

On her return to the nest, the female inserts her bill into one of her youngsters' gaping mouths, bringing the nectar up from the crop, and literally pumps it into the little one's throat! All observers who have watched this procedure agree that it is a terrifying spectacle, especially if the birds involved happen to be members of a very long-billed species, for the mother inserts her needlelike bill to such a depth into the baby's throat that the nervous observer expects at any moment the point to pierce the little one's body and

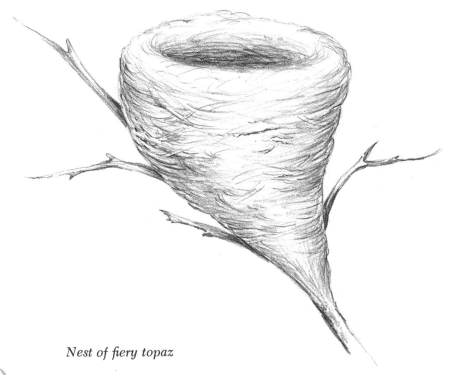

Nest of fiery topaz

Brooding female black-chinned hummingbird

come through on the other side. Evidently, however, accidents like that never happen; mama hummingbird safely withdraws her bill from the mouth of her temporarily satisfied youngster, and flies off to collect the next meal. On her return to the nest, the sword-swallowing act is performed all over again.

During the entire period of nest-building, incubating, and raising the young, the natural fearlessness and fighting spirit of the hummingbirds become even more pronounced. Let any animal, even a large one, seem to threaten the nest and its young, and the mother will attack it with unparalleled fury. Hummingbirds have been observed driving away hawks a hundred times their own size!

The time needed by the young to develop to the point where

they can leave the nest varies a good deal, even among members of the same species. It has been observed, for instance, that in some cases the young of ruby-throated hummingbirds were ready to fly within a period of ten days. Other young ruby-throats, on the other hand, took a full month to reach that stage. It is believed that the amount of food the mother can find for the young plays an important part in the rate of their development.

The two scrawny hummingbird youngsters have to be fed dozens of liquid meals a day.

Young hummingbirds are fed by mother who inserts her bill into the baby's throat and pumps nectar into its stomach.

The young, male as well as female, look very much like the female for quite some time after they leave the nest. That means that they have generally duller colors and little iridescence. The glittering metallic iridescence that distinguishes the plumage of the adult male is acquired much later, after the first molt, or shedding of feathers, which takes place about a year after the birds have hatched.

A little while after they leave the nest, the young hummingbirds are already fully able to take care of themselves, and with that moment all their native characteristics appear. Fearless, curious, and quick-tempered, these greenhorn youngsters will give chase to other animals considered by them to be intruders, investigate anything that catches their fancy, and engage in battles with others of their kind—not excluding their own mother—which they appear to consider a thoroughly enjoyable sport. In spite of their sharply pointed bills, hummingbirds do not seem to hurt each other during these air battles, even though they often collide with great force. Small as they are, their skin is leatherstrong, and difficult to pierce.

In time, the young hummingbirds will become fully adult, the young males will shed the dull feathers of their adolescence, grow the resplendent, glittering plumage of adulthood, and be ready to court, dazzle, and win females who then go about raising future generations of hummingbirds.

Hummingbirds on the Wing

The bird world is famous for the elegant, graceful, and seemingly tireless flight performances of many of its members. Even among this group of expert fliers, however, the tiny hummingbird is unique. Not a single other kind of bird can match or duplicate this little bird's mode of flying. While other birds fly forward, and have to turn their body if they want to change the direction of their flight, a hummingbird need not do anything of the kind. It can fly sideways, backwards, straight up and down—in fact, practically in any direction it wants to. In addition, the hummingbird can hover in mid-air, its body motionless, like a tiny helicopter.

The exact details of how and why the hummingbird can achieve this unmatched mastery of the air long remained a mystery because of the speed with which it moves in flight. Modern high-

40

speed cameras finally have provided the instrument for "freezing" the flight of the hummingbird, thus replacing speculation with exact knowledge of how these tiny birds manage to perform their astonishing aerial acrobatics, which have intrigued generations of naturalists.

The basis for their specialized flight is the peculiar wing structure of the hummingbirds. The wing muscles are huge in comparison to the size of the bird. They take up more than one-fourth of the entire body weight and are, relatively, the largest in the entire animal kingdom. Attached to a long breastbone, these muscles supply the strength for the hummingbird's wing action. The wings have no flexible joints at the points that would correspond to the elbow and wrist in human beings. In fact, still speaking in terms of the human arm, the wings are almost all "hand." The shoulder joints, however, are flexible in the extreme—so much so that they can be turned almost 180 degrees, which means that the wing can be twisted upside down, until the inner surface is turned toward

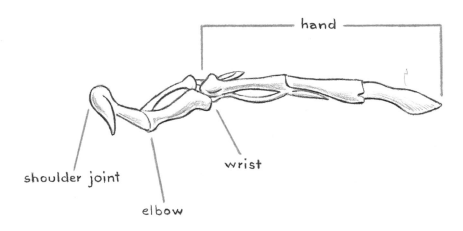

Bone structure of a hummingbird's wing

41

the outside. In other words, the hummingbird's wings are some-what like stiff paddles attached to the shoulders by joints of rub-bery flexibility, thus permitting the wing to pivot. In some ways, hummingbird wings thus can be compared more closely to the wings of insects than to those of other birds.

Because of the special construction of their wings, humming-birds get twice as much flying power as other birds. Although de-tails of their flight are very complex, the basic mechanics can be readily understood, especially if one keeps in mind the similarity of its hovering flight to the flight of a helicopter.

We are all familiar with the high maneuverability of the heli-copter as compared to the conventional type of airplane. A plane

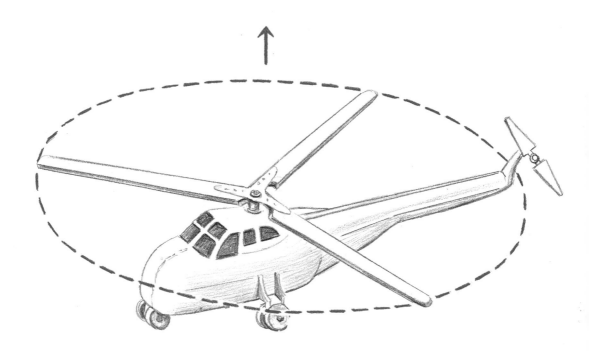

Rotating blades of helicopter lift the ma-chine by pushing down stream of air.

Hummingbird's wings, pivoting on shoulder joints, allow the bird to hover like a tiny helicopter.

not only needs a runway for takeoff, or for landing, but also can fly in only one direction—forward. A helicopter, on the other hand, is capable of rising straight up into the air, hovering in one spot, and landing vertically. In addition, it can fly sideways and backwards. All this is accomplished with the help of propeller blades which revolve around a vertical axis. The reaction of the stream of air driven downward by the rapidly rotating blades lifts and supports the helicopter in the air. When the machine hovers, the blades rotate on a horizontal plane, parallel to the ground.

Very much the same thing happens when a hummingbird hovers. Its wings pivot on the flexible shoulder joints, moving backward and forward at a rate of about 50 times a second. Backward movement is achieved by tilting the wings backward, with the body then in an almost vertical position.

The tail plays an important part in the hummingbird's flight. It

By tilting wings, hummingbirds can fly backward.

is constantly being spread, closed, tilted, cupped, and even angled during the various phases of flight. The changing position of the tail in the blast of air created by the wings has much to do with

44

*Full speed ahead—at
30 miles per hour*

the bird's extreme maneuverability, and its capacity to fly in all directions.

The characteristic humming sound is usually not heard when the bird hovers, as is commonly believed, but rather when the bird flies full speed ahead. As to the maximum speed that can be achieved by the hummingbird, as well as the rate of its wingbeats,

*Tail helps hummingbird to achieve
great maneuverability.*

One of the smallest of all hummingbirds, Calliphlox
amethystina, *beats its wings 80 times per second.*

differences of opinion exist even between experts. A maximum
speed of 50 miles per hour is frequently attributed to the bird, but
recent thorough studies seem to prove that the top speed—unless
aided by a tail wind—is closer to 30 than to 50 miles per hour.

As for the rate of wingbeat, careful and extensive studies of
many different hummingbirds have resulted in some interesting
statistics. It was long assumed that all hummingbirds had an extremely rapid wingbeat. This, however, is not quite true. It seems
that the frequency of wingbeat depends on the *size* of the bird—
the smaller the bird, the faster it beats its wings; the larger the
bird, the slower the rate. One very small hummingbird has been
clocked at 80 strokes per second, while the giant hummingbird of
the Andes makes only about 10 strokes per second. The latter, by
the way, is the least efficient when it comes to hovering.

Whatever future study and observations may yield in new de-
tails of hummingbird flight techniques, rate of speed and wingbeat, it cannot alter the fact that these little birds have developed
a mode of flight that makes them superior in maneuverability to all
other members of the bird clan. Watching a hummingbird on the
wing is to receive a lesson in what Nature can achieve in the field

of aerodynamics. This should help to keep us from getting too proud of our own inventions in this field. Our helicopter, for instance, is a wonderful machine; but Nature's helicopter, the hummingbird, can match the flight of a mechanical helicopter in every way—and does it on only half the fuel in proportion to its weight! In addition, it must be admitted that when it comes to appearances, the vote goes to the hummingbird every time, for it adds beauty to efficiency in a perfectly balanced combination.

The Hummingbirds of North America

At first glance, the number of different kinds of hummingbirds found in the United States—about 15 in all—seems like quite a lot. On the strength of the number alone, one could be tempted to believe that hummingbirds are fairly abundant all over the country. This, however, is not so. The total number is misleading because the majority of these species is confined to just the southwestern parts of the United States. Some, indeed, are found only in regions along the U.S.-Mexican border. Actually, there are only two kinds of hummingbirds that are found over wide parts of the North American continent: the ruby-throated hummingbird in the East, and the rufous hummingbird west of the Mississippi. These two, however, have an enormously wide range. Ruby-throats breed as far north as Labrador and Newfoundland, and the rufous hummingbird even goes up to Alaska. The only parts of the continent not frequented by these hummingbirds are the regions in which no flowers are found.

The ruby-throat, a common visitor to the gardens of eastern United States, is a three-inch bird with a bill that measures about one-fourth of the total body length. The male does justice to the species' name, for it has a glowing deep red "bib." Head and back are metallic golden green, breast and belly grayish white. The female, lacking the red throat, is all white below. The tail feathers in both species are blackish, tipped with white in the female.

Seeing for the first time a ruby-throat darting from flower to flower, its wings beating so rapidly that they appear as a blur, the layman many easily mistake the bird for one of the large moths,

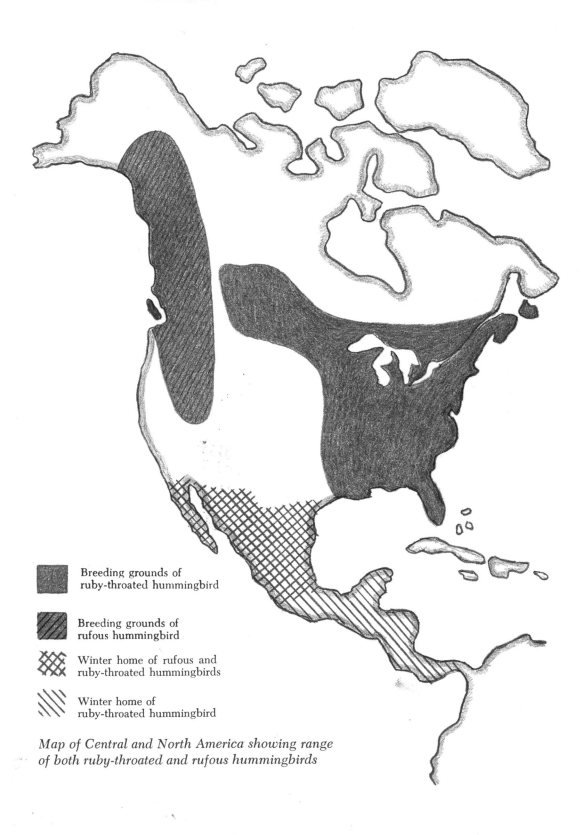

Breeding grounds of
ruby-throated hummingbird

Breeding grounds of
rufous hummingbird

Winter home of rufous and
ruby-throated hummingbirds

Winter home of
ruby-throated hummingbird

*Map of Central and North America showing range
of both ruby-throated and rufous hummingbirds*

Ruby-throat (left) and rufous hummingbird

especially because hummingbirds like to fly in the dusk, and the whirring noises caused by the bird's wing motion sound much like those made by some moths. The red throat of the male is often hardly visible, partly because the bird moves so rapidly, partly because the light has to be just right for the color to show up— from certain angles the throat may appear almost black.

The "little star," Stellula calliope, *is found in California.*

Looking at the tiny bird as it flits around in our gardens, it seems hard to realize that it took the little fellow a 2,000-mile trip to get here. The winter home of the ruby-throat is Central America, often as far south as Panama. To reach its breeding grounds in North America, it has to migrate every year in the spring, covering more than 2,000 miles, and then make the same return trip in the fall. This amazing journey includes a flight of 500 miles across the Gulf of Mexico, during which the bird can neither eat nor sleep, or even rest.

The broadtail occurs in southwestern United States.

The question of how so tiny a bird gets the energy to make so long and strenuous a non-stop flight has been answered through patient study and observation by naturalists. They found that nature has given the ruby-throat the ability to store large amounts of fat against the extra energy output demanded by its migration. Before starting on the long journey, the bird fattens up by regularly consuming larger amounts of food, and in this way adds about 50 per cent to its weight within a relatively short period. All this extra weight is pure fat, which can be used as fuel for the exertions required during migration. To realize what this means, imagine a human being trying to do the same thing. A person weighing 150 pounds would have to add, in a few weeks' time, an extra 75 pounds of fat to his weight—fat which he would lose again just as quickly because he would have to go without food or sleep for many days.

After arriving at their destination in the United States—or Canada, whichever it may be—the ruby-throated hummingbirds visit gardens and other flower beds for their daily meals, build nests, and raise their young. Then, when summer fades and fall comes, the birds, including the young who have never made the trip before, wing their way south to their winter quarters in Central America.

In the West, the rufous hummingbird takes the place of the ruby-throat. It is just about the same size as the eastern species, but differs in coloring, being bright reddish above instead of green. The throat of the male is flame red, more orange in hue than that of the ruby-throat.

The rufous hummingbird also is a great migrant, covering about the same distance as does its eastern relative, although it does not have to cross vast stretches of water. Found all over the western part of the North American continent, the rufous hummingbird has been observed to breed as far north as 60 degrees latitude in Alaska.

The third migratory North American hummingbird is the tiny calliope. It does not, however, cover anywhere near the distance traveled by the other two. The full scientific name of this bird is

*The blue-throat likes
to live near water.*

Stellula calliope, which translated means "beautiful-voiced little star." While the first part of the name—little star—is well-chosen in view of the star-shaped collar of reddish-purple iridescent feathers worn by the male, the second part is definitely a misnomer. Far from having a beautiful voice, the calliope, like all other humming-birds, lacks true singing ability, and by no stretch of the imagination can the chattering, chipping noises it makes be considered a beautiful melody.

The calliope winters in Mexico, and migrates north to south-western United States, especially California. The handsome broad-bill is another species of the American Southwest. The male of the species has a bright red bill, and an iridescent emerald green underside. It lives in the mountains of Mexico, New Mexico, and Arizona.

The broadtail, another mountain-dwelling species, has a range that extends from Guatemala to Wyoming. It looks somewhat like the ruby-throat, with a bright red metallic throat. The outstanding feature of this hummingbird is the form of the large wing feathers, which are tapered in the male, resulting in slots between the individual feathers. When the bird is in flight, air is forced through these spaces, causing a shrill whistling noise.

One of the largest of all hummingbirds found in North America is the blue-throat. It is not a very brilliant bird as hummingbirds go, the iridescence being confined mainly to a throat patch of blue worn by the male. The blue-throat lives in Mexico and the American Southwest—Arizona, Texas, and New Mexico. It likes water and is frequently seen near streams and waterfalls.

Wherever they turn up, however, be it east or west, north or south, hummingbirds are always welcome guests, gladly greeted as they flit from flower to flower, colorful, gay, and fearless. Anyone who observes these charming little birds will most likely agree with the extravagant praise that has been heaped upon these "fragments of the rainbow" by expert and layman alike.

Attracting Hummingbirds to Your Garden

While it is interesting to hear or read about hummingbirds and their habits, it cannot compare with actually watching these little birds as they probe flowers for nectar, darting from blossom to blossom in their pursuit of the sweet liquid.

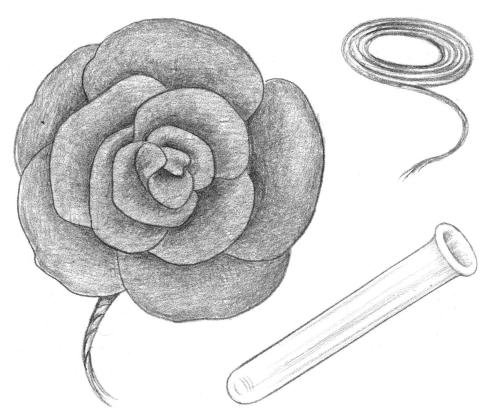

Materials for construction of an artificial hummingbird feeder

*Morning glory and columbine are among
blossoms that attract hummingbirds.*

Almost any garden or backyard that has flowering shrubs or
bushes, or tall, showy flowers, may expect to have hummingbirds
visiting it sooner or later. These birds are attracted especially by
the blossoms of trumpet vine, honeysuckle, and morning glory.
Among flowers, delphinium, columbine, bellflower and cardinal
flower seem to be favorites.

Even if your backyard or garden does not have these flowers,
however, you do not need to give up all hope of having hummingbird visitors, for you can make artificial feeders that have a good
chance of attracting the little birds. These feeders are very inex-
pensive and easy to construct.

Red, as we have seen, seems to be the favorite color of hummingbirds. Therefore, your feeder should show a large amount of
red. Buy a large, bright red or orange red plastic flower. Then take
a small glass test tube, and wire it to the flower in a way so that
the opening will protrude slightly from under the edge of the plastic leaves. The accompanying drawing will show you how to do

this. Then, fasten the flower with the attached test tube to a bush in a location where the feeder can be easily seen from any direction. Do not choose a spot too high up in the bush—you will want to be able to watch comfortably when the bird comes along, and therefore a location at about eye level would be ideal.

The flower should be fastened in a way that will cause the tube to be tilted slightly, as shown in the second drawing, so that the opening points upwards. Now your feeder is ready to be filled. Prepare a mixture of sugar and water, using about two teaspoonfuls of sugar for a half cup of water, and making sure that the sugar is well dissolved. Fill the feeder tube almost to the rim. You will have to replenish the evaporated water from time to time, filling the tube with fresh sugar water every week or so.

sugar water

The finished hummingbird feeder

57

Now you are ready to watch and see if your feeder will attract any hummingbirds. You can expect to see them especially on summer days when dusk is just beginning to set in. If you see one, do not hesitate to watch it from close up, for hummingbirds are not shy—if one of these birds has made up its mind to examine your feeder for food, it will not be deterred by any human being who happens to be standing nearby. You should, of course, avoid hasty and sudden movements.

58

Even if you do succeed in attracting hummingbirds to your garden with the help of the artificial feeder, do not expect to see immediately the glittering colors for which these birds are famous. Your visitor, for instance, may be a female, a relatively dull-colored bird. Even the males, however, do not always show the characteristic iridescence, for during flight these areas are often not visible

because the light has to come from exactly the right angle to make them show up. If you are patient, though, you may one day be lucky enough to see the brilliant flash of a fiery red throat. In any case, your success in having attracted these charming birds to your garden, and in being able to watch them hover before the feeder as they suck the sugar water you prepared for them, will prove an exciting and rewarding experience.

Index

Pages on which illustrations appear are printed in italics.

ABOUT THE AUTHOR-ARTIST

Hilda Simon's concern for perfection of detail in her illustrations is matched only by her interest in animal and insect life. Born in California, Miss Simon spent many years in Europe, where she went to school and later studied art. Even as a small child, she was fascinated by animal life in all its forms and always had what amounted to a small zoo at home, which at times presented a problem for her parents because of the rattlesnakes and scorpions that invaded the gardens in California.

She studied and raised various animals and insects, from frogs, lizards, and mice to butterflies, beetles, and honeybees. The fearlessness of the tiny hummingbirds that nested in the family rose garden especially intrigued her, and these colorful and acrobatic birds have been a source of wonder and delight ever since. Her collection of sketches and drawings, many of which she has used as illustration material in her nature books, includes numerous ones of hummingbirds.

Miss Simon now lives in New York City. Titles she has written and illustrated include EXPLORING THE WORLD OF SOCIAL INSECTS and WONDERS OF THE BUTTERFLY WORLD, as well as the present volume, WONDERS OF HUMMINGBIRDS.